INFLUENTIAL

WOMEN IN ENGINEERING

EMMA KAISER

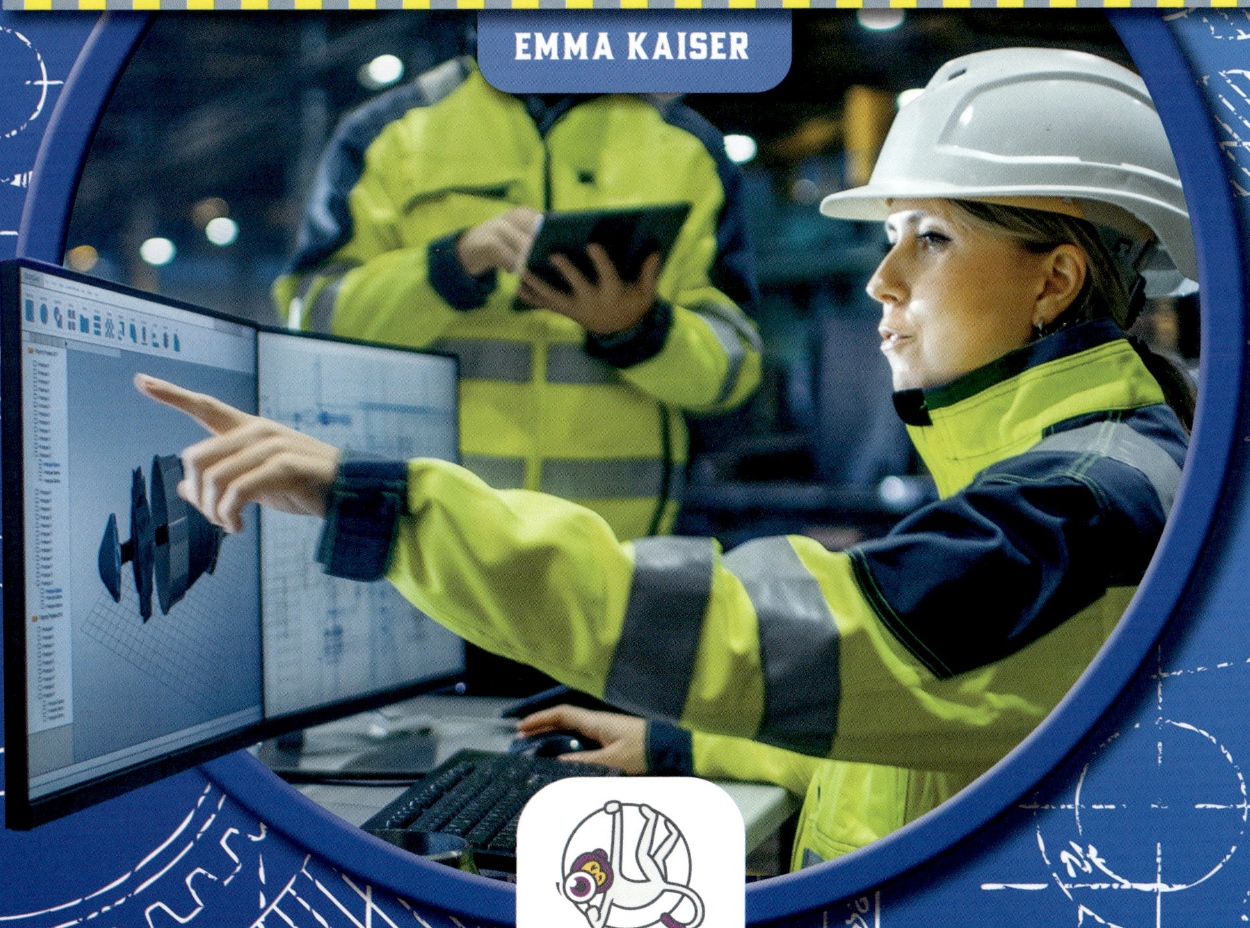

childsworld.com

Published by The Child's World®
800-599-READ · www.childsworld.com

Photography Credits
Photographs ©: Shutterstock Images, cover (engineer), 1 (engineer), 18–19; Jason Winter/Shutterstock Images, cover (background), 1 (background), 3 (background); Alexander Skowalsky/Noun Project, cover (icon), 1 (icon), 3 (icon), back cover; Science History Images/Alamy, 5; Sundry Photography/Shutterstock Images, 7; Pixabay, 9; Rosemarie Mosteller/Shutterstock Images, 10–11; Bob Nye/NASA, 13, 15; Sarah Silbiger/Bloomberg/Getty Images, 17; Red Line Editorial, 20

ISBN Information
9781503889583 (Reinforced Library Binding)
9781503890268 (Portable Document Format)
9781503891500 (Online Multi-user eBook)
9781503892743 (Electronic Publication)

LCCN 2023950454

Printed in the United States of America

Emma Kaiser is a writer and educator based in western Minnesota. She has a master of fine arts (MFA) in creative writing from the University of Minnesota, and her writing has appeared in a number of magazines and publications. She is the author of several other nonfiction books for students.

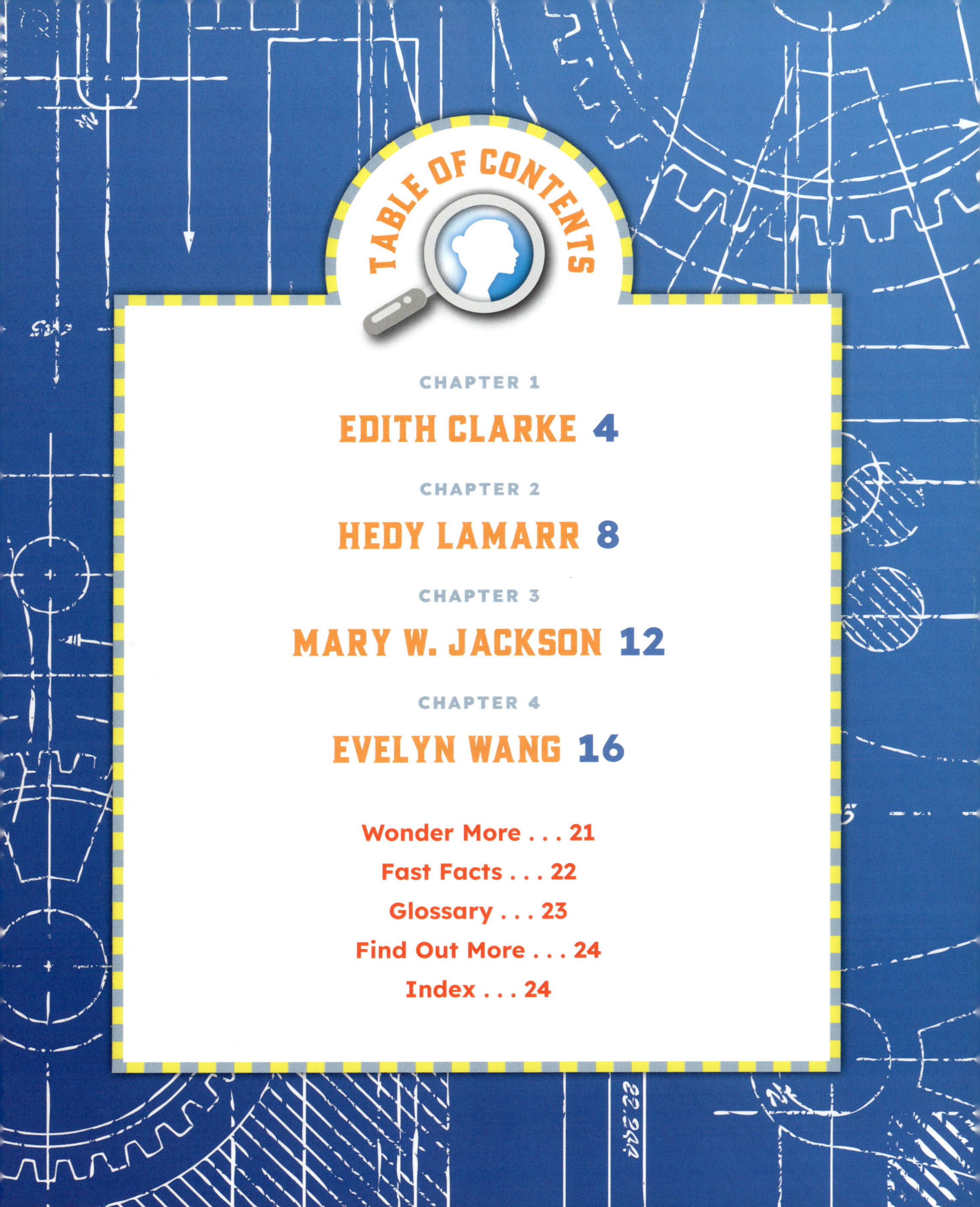

TABLE OF CONTENTS

EDITH CLARKE

Edith Clarke was born in Maryland in 1883. Both her parents died by the time she was 12 years old. She used the money they left her to attend Vassar College. She studied mathematics and **astronomy**. She graduated in 1908. For a time, she worked as a teacher. In 1918, she enrolled at the Massachusetts Institute of Technology (MIT).

In 1921, Clarke taught physics in the country of Turkey.

At MIT, Clarke earned a master of science degree in electrical **engineering**. She was the first woman to earn that degree from MIT. But many companies did not want to hire a female engineer. She eventually took a job at General Electric in the state of New York. Her job was to do mathematical **calculations**. But she also invented a new kind of calculator. Electrical engineers could use the calculator to solve problems with power lines.

In 1922, Clarke became a **salaried** electrical engineer at General Electric. She published a lot of important papers. She also wrote textbooks on electrical engineering.

General Electric was founded by Thomas Edison and others in 1892.

Clarke later became the first female professor of electrical engineering in the United States. Then, in 1954, she earned an award from the Society of Women Engineers. After she died, she was added to the National Inventors Hall of Fame.

HEDY LAMARR

In 1914, Hedy Lamarr was born in Austria. She moved to the United States in 1937. She worked as an actress in Hollywood. She starred in many popular movies. But acting wasn't her only interest. She loved to tinker with machines.

World War II (1939–1945) began in Europe. Lamarr wanted to help. She partnered with a man named George Antheil. They invented a new communication system. It was based on radio technology.

Lamarr starred in movies such as *Boom Town* and *I Take This Woman.*

Lamarr called it the Secret Communication System. She sent her invention to the navy. She hoped it would help them control weapons from far away.

The navy did not take Lamarr's invention. They didn't think it would work. Years later, the navy would change their minds. In the 1960s, they used Lamarr's invention to send secret messages.

Lamarr did not receive much credit for her work until later in life. She never made any money for her invention. But her work later made Wi-Fi possible. Wi-Fi uses radio waves to connect devices to the internet without using wires. In 2014, Lamarr was added to the National Inventors Hall of Fame.

Every year, the National Inventors Hall of Fame celebrates the contributions of important engineers.

MARY W. JACKSON

Many early Black female engineers did not become well-known until after they died. Mary W. Jackson was one of these engineers. She was born in 1921 in Virginia. She graduated from high school with highest honors. Then she went to the Hampton Institute. She earned degrees in mathematics and physical science in 1942.

In 1951, Jackson began working for the National Advisory Committee for **Aeronautics** (NACA). She worked for their computing unit with other Black female mathematicians.

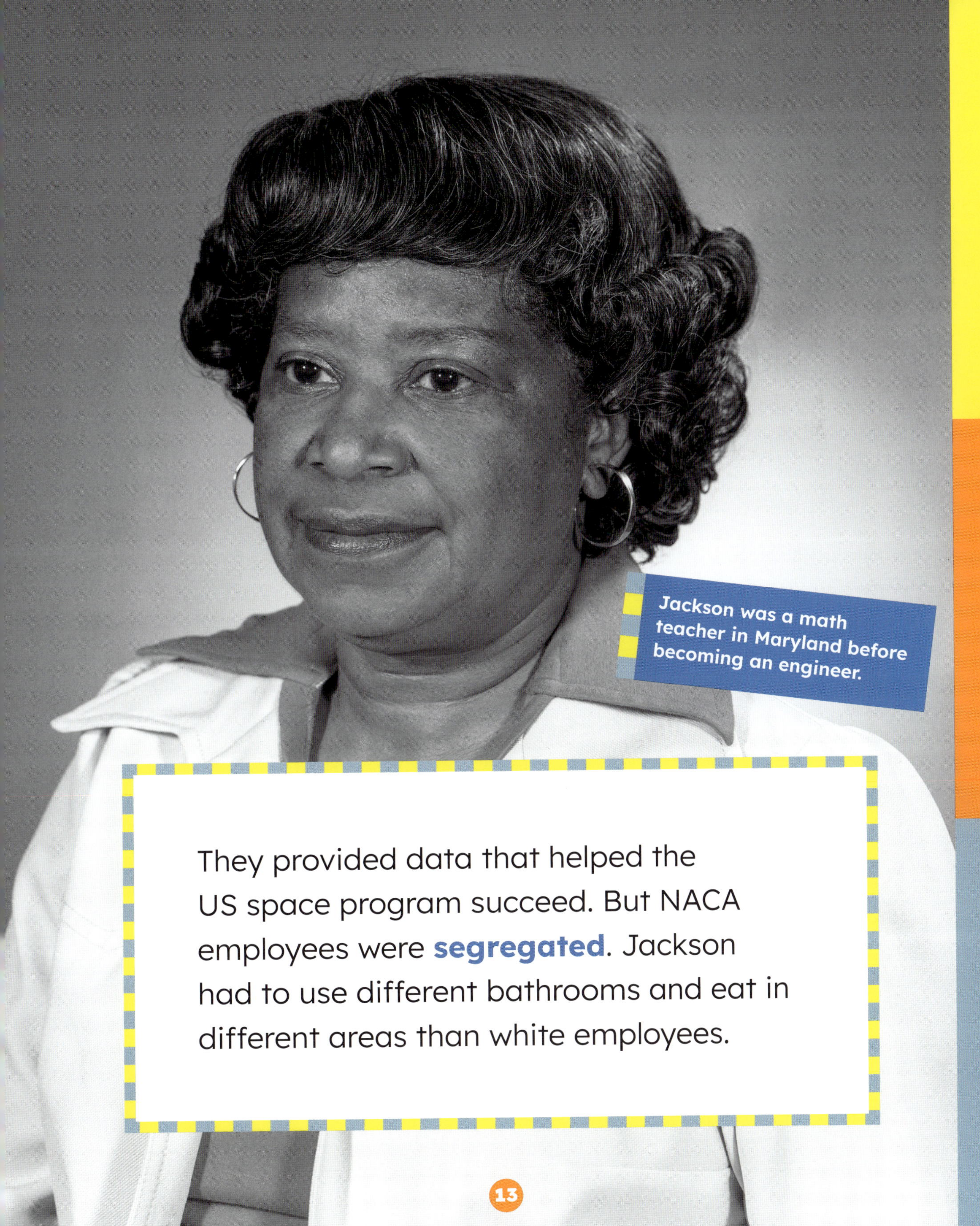

Jackson was a math teacher in Maryland before becoming an engineer.

They provided data that helped the US space program succeed. But NACA employees were **segregated**. Jackson had to use different bathrooms and eat in different areas than white employees.

Jackson decided she wanted to become an engineer. She attended a training program at the University of Virginia. In 1958, NACA became the National Aeronautics and Space Administration (NASA). That year, Jackson became the first Black female engineer at NASA. She worked as an aerospace engineer for more than 20 years. Aerospace engineers work on aircraft and spacecraft. Jackson studied how air flowed around NASA aircrafts. But she was never given higher engineering roles.

In 1979, Jackson left her role as an engineer. She went to manage the NASA women's program. She led more female mathematicians and engineers to join NASA. She retired from NASA in 1985. She died in 2005. In 2019, Jackson was awarded the Congressional Gold Medal.

Jackson tested the flow of air around objects in wind tunnels.

HIDDEN FIGURES

There were other Black women who worked on NASA's space program. They included mathematicians Dorothy Vaughan and Katherine Johnson. A 2016 book called *Hidden Figures* told the story of their work at NASA. That same year, the book was made into a movie.

EVELYN WANG

Evelyn Wang was born in the state of New York to Taiwanese parents. Her parents had met as students at the Massachusetts Institute of Technology (MIT). They encouraged her in school and music. Wang grew up playing the piano and the violin. But she discovered that she was truly passionate about engineering.

Wang followed in her parents' footsteps. She also attended MIT. She earned a degree in mechanical engineering.

Wang has written many important papers in her career.

Then she went to Stanford University. She earned higher degrees there. In 2007, Wang went back to MIT as a teacher. She taught mechanical engineering. She later became the head of MIT's mechanical engineering department.

Solar panels capture energy from sunlight and turn it into electricity.

Wang has studied how heat moves among materials. Her work might improve the **efficiency** of some machines. Wang is especially interested in solar energy. This is energy that comes from the sun. Solar energy technology can help with issues such as climate change. Climate change is the warming of Earth and changing of weather caused by human activities.

Wang helped design a device that pulls water out of the air in dry climates. She also helped create a system that removes salt from sea water. These devices could provide people with clean drinking water.

WOMEN IN ARCHITECTURE AND ENGINEERING IN THE UNITED STATES

Though the number of women in engineering and related fields has increased over the years, there is still progress to be made.

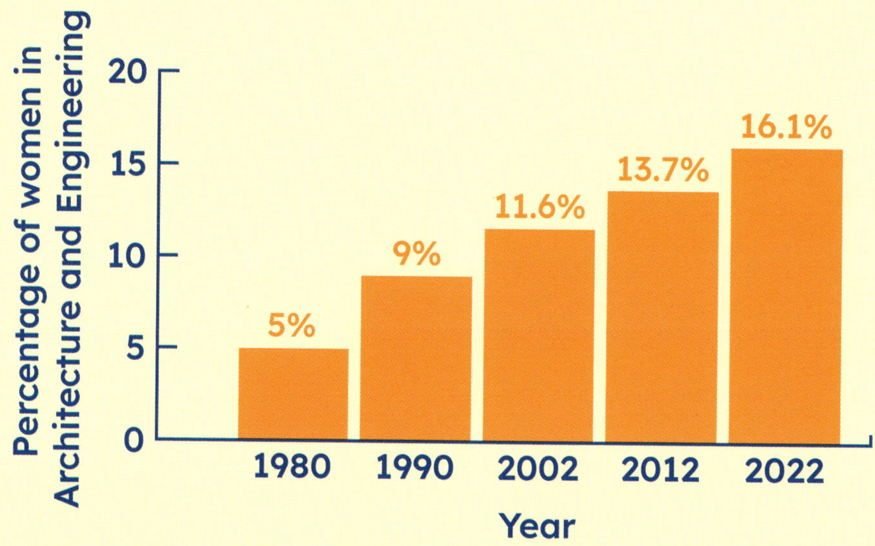

Wang has won many important awards and **grants**. In 2022, President Joe Biden chose Wang to lead a branch within the US Department of Energy. She remains a leader in engineering.

WONDER MORE

Wondering about New Information

How much did you know about women in engineering before reading this book? What new information did you learn? Write down three facts that this book taught you. Was the new information surprising? Why or why not?

Wondering How It Matters

What is one way engineering relates to your life? If you cannot think of a personal connection, imagine a way the topic might affect other kids. What impact might it have on their lives?

Wondering Why

Many important inventions and advancements are the result of female engineers. Why do you think it is important for people to know about them and their work? Do you think it changes the way people think about their work?

Ways to Keep Wondering

Engineering is a complex topic. After reading this book, what questions do you have about it? What can you do to learn more about women in engineering?

FAST FACTS

- Women have made significant contributions in the field of engineering. But some of their work is not as well-known or recognized.
- Edith Clarke was the first woman to earn a master's degree in electrical engineering from MIT. She was also the first woman to be a professor of electrical engineering.
- Clarke invented a calculator that helped electrical engineers.
- Hedy Lamarr created radio technology that helped the US Navy. But she was neither recognized nor paid for her invention.
- Lamarr's invention would eventually make Wi-Fi technology possible.
- Female engineers of color faced additional barriers in their field.
- Mary W. Jackson was a Black engineer who helped establish NASA's space program. She was denied higher roles, but she helped create opportunities for other women.
- Women still represent a small percentage of engineers. But women such as Evelyn Wang are becoming influential leaders.
- Wang was appointed to lead a branch of the Department of Energy in 2022.

GLOSSARY

aeronautics (ayr-oh-NOT-iks) Aeronautics is the study of traveling through air. Mary W. Jackson worked in the field of aeronautics.

astronomy (uh-STRON-uh-mee) Astronomy is the study of outer space. Edith Clarke studied astronomy at Vassar College.

calculations (kal-kyu-LAY-shuns) Calculations are mathematical ways of solving a problem to get an answer. Edith Clarke performed calculations in her job at General Electric.

efficiency (uh-FISH-un-see) Efficiency is the ability to avoid waste. Engineers commonly aim for efficiency in their creations.

engineering (en-juh-NEER-ing) Engineering is the field of designing and building structures or machines such as engines. The number of women in engineering is increasing.

grants (GRANTZ) Grants are sums of money given to someone for a specific purpose. Evelyn Wang has earned several grants in her career.

salaried (SAL-uh-reed) A salaried job is one for which the employee receives a steady, periodic payment. Edith Clarke was a salaried employee of General Electric.

segregated (SEH-gruh-gay-ted) Something is segregated if it is divided by race. Many American schools and workplaces were segregated between Black and white people in the 1900s.

FIND OUT MORE

In the Library

Rathburn, Betsy. *Electrical Engineer.* Minneapolis, MN: Bellwether, 2023.

Smibert, Angie. *Engineering.* Parker, CO: The Child's World, 2021.

Washington, Danni. *Bold Women in Science: 15 Women in History You Should Know.* Emeryville, CA: Rockridge Press, 2021.

On the Web

Visit our website for links about women in engineering:
childsworld.com/links

Note to Parents, Caregivers, Teachers, and Librarians: We routinely verify our web links to make sure they are safe and active sites. So encourage your readers to check them out!

INDEX